love, and you

gretchen gomez

love, and you
copyright © 2017 by gretchen gomez

All rights reserved.
Cover Art: Islam Farid
islamfarid.net

Editor: Lilly Lozada (my book twin)
https://lairofbooksblog.wordpress.com

First Edition
ISBN-10: 1542662958
ISBN-13: 978-1542662956

dedication

to the guy who
was once my
anchor,

sorry that our
sail wasn't very
smooth.

to the women who
know they
deserve better,

this one's for you.

loving you was
one of the
g r e a t e s t
experiences
of my life

because i finally
learned how to
love myself

when
you
didn't
know
how
to

my father once
told me

"deja de escucharlo
  y mira lo que el
  hace por ti.
    ¿que te a probado?
  nada."

"stop listening to
  him and look
  to see what he
  does for you.
  what has he proved to you?
  nothing."

my mother
told me

"mira la situación
 de el,
 ¿a cambiado?
 no.
 tu eres demasiado inteligente
 para eso;
 yo no te puedo verte a ti
 arrastrándote por ese hoyo de nuevo."

"look at his
 situation,
 has he changed?
 no.
 you're too smart
 for that;
 I can't see you
 crawl in that hole again."

i once dreamt that
i kept getting on and off
the wrong trains and
never found my stop.

i felt scared.

once i got off the
right stop, i felt
like i was walking
in the wrong direction.

when i woke up
from that dream,
i felt marked and hollow.
and i thought
about myself and
what i was doing
in the dream.

here's what i learned:
- i never looked at the signs
  when getting on and off the train
- i didn't feel at peace when
  i got off the right stop

the right stop is my
heart loving you.
but we were always headed
in the wrong direction
because we were too busy
being on and off,
that i never looked
at the signs
my father warned me about.

i should've stopped
all of this when
i realized that i was
the other woman
to your family.

and they would
never stop comparing
me to her, your ex.

and you weren't
anyone to give
me my place.

- i shouldn't beg for respect

i also should've
stopped this
when i tried
cleaning your
daughters face
and she told me
to stop acting like
her mommy.

i told her that
i just wanted
to be her friend.
and friends don't
let each other
look dirty.

i should've stopped
when we were at
a get together
at your friends house

and i was
three feet away
when your friend
asked you
about your ex.

and
you
answered.

without giving me my place

- *again.*

tag, you're it.
a game he played
with a girl he
once dated.

back and forth
follow to unfollow
follow to unfollow
follow to unfollow

then he started following all these girls
breaking
my
trust
with
each
follow.

till he told his little friend how much he missed
her while everyone was watching.

i felt like he mentally cheated on me.

deja vu:
all my previous relationships.
asking myself if i was
enough for him.

- my insecurities are the demons that never go away

i
should've
stopped
when
you
never
called
me
on
my
birthday.

and when you left me
in pain with a broken heart.
knowing damn well
what you did to me.
you left me bleeding.
but you were too busy
getting on a flight,
having the time of your life.

- abandonment issues

my abandonment issues
never left, they started
from a very young age.

he had triggered
some of the worst
parts of my mind.

he never showed
up when i needed
him the most.

once i realized that
he had abandoned
me from time to time,

i
never
wanted
to
flee
so
fast.

i was going to see a therapist
after not seeing one for 10+ years.
there were things i had been through
between those years, and things
that 15 year old me never discussed
when i was seeing one at the time.
the wreckage of my body since
the age of 6.

i was ready to set myself free
from every single fucking demon
that tormented me.

the night before the session,
i was stricken with anxiety.
i ran to the bathroom so many
times and i asked him to be
there for me, at least the day
of the appointment.
he never showed, before or after.
or even the day after.

i was on a long train ride home
revisiting all my old memories
without anyone to hold.
i felt so abandoned and alone.

i needed him to bang
on my door and
scream an apology.

fill me with love in person.

i needed him to
physically be there
and show his sorries.

i didn't need flowers
i didn't need fruits
i didn't need books
sent
from
another
carrier.

i needed him in person
telling me that he fucked up
and he wasn't going to
leave till i accepted his apology.

after all,
what
the
fuck
am i supposed
to do with a
half assed
text message
that states
"I'm sorry for hurting you"?

- fucking asshole

advice:
if someone is always
in and out your life,
then you leave.
you deserve stability.

if that person isn't there
for you the countless times
you needed, run the other way.
you deserve someone
who will stay.

i still
don't understand
how someone can
chase another being
for two years.

and when the other
being says yes.

that someone
isn't ready.

so why fucking chase me?

you weren't prepared for me?
no i honestly wasn't.
what's your plan with me?
i don't know.

i'm not an i don't know plan.
i'm a forever plan.

i wanted to kiss him deeply
till he tasted all of my rage.

caress him till he felt my pain,
tingling all over his body.

look him in the eyes till his
bones trembled with my agony.

and it still wouldn't have been enough...

star light,
star bright,
please stop this aching heart of *mine*

- and that didn't happen

i hated the
thought
of losing you

because i thought
no one would
understand me
love me
see me
mentally get me
the way you do.

but
i
was
losing
myself

while still trying to be with you.

i felt so fucked up.
as if death was
trying to have an
early visitation,
reminding me
of all the wrongs
in my life.

I've stood stock-still between the lines of normal and psychotic. Then one day I had one foot on normal and the other foot on psychotic.

I fear insanity wrapping me in a blanket every single day. Because I know what it taste like
When
Each
Corner
Of
Your
Mind
Becomes
Hollow.

then you become this person
imprisoned
in
your
small
hollowed
mind.

And you don't know where you are because
You're
In
Five
Places
At
The
Same
Goddamnfuckingtime.
And your mind is constantly drunk on insanity.

- my mind is my worst enemy

i once told him that
there were things i
most likely would
never forgive him for.

me not knowing
that i had to
forgive myself,
in order to heal
from the wounds
he gave me.

me also not knowing
that i had to simply
forgive because all
of this could've been
avoided, had i left
sooner rather than later.

i
don't
know
how
to
write
about
the
happy
parts

                              because
                                  all
                                    i
                                 knew
                                  was
                                  the
                              sadness

the air i breathed.
he stood still for
me when i was all
over the place.

- the anchor to my raging sea

he completed the
thoughts inside my head.
not my sentences.

my
thoughts

- he understood my silence

he loves me.
i know he does.

the look in his eyes,
the way he tries.

resentment came
to visit a few times.

there was an aroma
of greatness from
the experienced
potential we once
danced in.

but
it
was
short
lived

and in spurts.

i can still smell his skin
all over the ridges of mine.

and he left an echo on
the parts of my skin he kissed.

he didn't know what he was doing
to my heart
to my soul

while he looked me in the eyes
and he said
i love you i love you i love you
i love you i love you i love you
and even while i cried
he kept telling me
i love you i love you i love you
i love you i love you i love you

and i smiled because
he took all my worry away.
he convinced me with
all those i love you's

that
love is real
love is mendable
love is me and him
wrapped in one.

and i love him
i love him
i love him
i love him

the
week
following,

he
didn't
prove
anything
to me.

- the sex is just that fucking great

his father....
his mother....

i
tried
to
make
excuses
for
his
behavior

                  but i can't make
                  excuses for a man
                  who doesn't know
                    what he wants.
                          not
                          just
                          for
                          me
                  but for himself.

i once thought that
had he cheated on me,
it would've made for a
great excuse to move on.

he
never
physically
cheated.

he didn't need
to cheat for me
to know that he
would never
understand my worth.

my worth is
not beneath
the land you
walk on

my worth is
more than
the time
you never
spent on me

my worth is
more than the
depression
that fights
to hug me

looking in the mirror
two years later

my eyes were so tired
of all the tears.

they said
no more
no more
no more.

i saw my skin,
the eczema reaction
due to the stress
and anxiety.

not even coconut oil could
take this heartache away.

i felt so empty
without him,
like a space
inside me was
waiting to be
filled by him again.

i found myself
so fucking tired
and exhausted
of living with
missing him.

i wish i could
travel to outer
space and find
another planet
to move away
from everything
that wrecks me.

my skin is boiled
with so many emotions,
words can't even do
it justice.

my doctor once asked
me what happened
with the relationship.

i explained to him
a little of the situation.

he told me:
1- never date a guy
who doesn't have
his head screwed
on right.
2- you shouldn't date
a guy with a kid,
you have too much
to see and a guy like
that is only going
to hold you back.

i
learned
my
lesson
when
i
felt
single
on
the
weekends

i was his girl monday thru friday

- balance

i blame that one on me.

love is an explosion
of vivid colors.

love is the unexplainable.

sometimes i think
that in this lifetime
we were meant to meet
just so we can get a taste.

and in another lifetime,
we're living happily
and we still talk about
the stars, the moon, the ocean.

and we live in the middle
of nowhere and it's just
me and him,

loving one another without limits.

we were dreamers
and reality washed
the dreams away
with all the
continuity of failures

- falling from cloud nine

one day he came
over to my house

and we cried for hours.

the tears spoke
for the silence
and the words
that were
never said.

he's an intelligent
human being

and his intelligence
frustrated me.

because i was
1st grade math

and he treated
me as if i
was calculus

- complexity in the simplest ways

the hurt
the anger
the madness

he
never
intended
to
do

he just didn't know
what to do
with a girl like me

and
with
that
came
the
downfall

victim:

i
can't
always
play.

there were
times i knew
exactly what i
was saying
and doing
to cause him pain.

- reciprocating toxins

i love him with words
i cannot express

nor my heart
and mind knows
how to say
what it wants to say

but i love him

deeper than the word love
crazier than he's ever seen
aching with all that's in me

i love him.

and there's no way around that

i once told him
i'd go through
everything again
to be with him.

~~physical abuse~~
~~emotional abuse~~
~~psychological abuse~~
~~abandonment~~
~~loss~~
~~hurt~~
~~rape~~
~~mistreatment~~
~~cancer~~
~~self harm~~
~~suicide attempts~~
~~usage~~
~~blackmail~~

~~every fucking thing that's ever happened to me.~~

what has become of me?

the best option
for my sanity
was to love you
from afar

i used to think
that humans were
crazy for letting
lovers affect them
so deeply.

till
i
lived
it.

the moon became
my best friend
and understood
all the tears
i shed.

- the girl who cried wolf

thoughts of me and him
had taken over my mind
all the time.

imagine the sky
as my mind
and my thoughts
are the stars.

- they were scattered all over the place

loving him
was so easy.

i was consumed by us
and what we could be.
it all started fantastic.
here, there, everywhere.

his lips soft,
his fingers that wrapped
around this broken skin.

he
made
me
feel
welcomed

people would tell
me to get over him
because it was
just a short time
of him in my life.

i wish they
understood that
it wasn't just
the time spent
together.

it was about
letting go of
the journeys
the future
the lifetime
we created.

there were so
many times
i had him right
next to me

and it's as
if he wasn't
there at all.

i breathed in
loneliness
and it swallowed
me deeper.

i was scared
to close my
eyes and sleep

because even in
my dreams he
was a nightmare.

there was no
escaping it,
regardless of
what i did.

so many times,
i told myself
in my sleep
get up
get up
get up, it's just a dream.

but was it?

waking up
in a haze
because
we didn't
make sense
anymore

- all the nightmares i told you about

inconsiderate:

when you ask them
to let go of you
and they don't.
knowing all the
hurt and damage
they're putting
you through.

you

        never

                considered

                        me

addiction
comes
in
different
forms

i was the addict.
he was the drug.

and every time i tried
to go into detox, he kept
coming back to me
with pretty hello's.

all the beautiful
memories came
with the withdrawals.

i always told
myself that i
didn't need
anyone in my life.

people
always
disappointed
me.

the hard truth
was that it had
also applied to him.

- a light bulb that turned on in this little mind

i knew things
weren't right
when i started
thinking about us,
and the memories
felt like they didn't
belong to me

but
to
a
stranger

- out of body experience

the cycle of us
was full of toxins
and filth.
on and off and on
and off and on and
off and spinning,
circling, like a carousel
round and round we go.
interchanging pain with
one another on and off
and on and off and on
and off.

i kissed him
    and tasted hope there

i kissed him
    and tasted love there

i kissed him
    and tasted years there

i kissed him
    and tasted sadness there

i kissed him
    and tasted nothing there

i kissed him
    and tasted myself there

i couldn't count
on his love
for me.
so i had started
loving myself.

i decided that the
only person who
was ever going to
disappoint and hurt
me was myself.

instead of getting
mad at him,
i got mad at
myself for staying.

the healing;
there were days
that i spent alone
crying out this
heartbreak.

my bones rattled
from the aching
of this heart.

my tears were
words my soul
had formed.

finally accepting
that there was
nothing i can
say or do
to make us stay.

i stopped digging graves
of our mess for you

it didn't make
sense to me
how we didn't
solve one another.

because our love
outranked
all
the
other
loves.

and yet he was
the worst one of
all because i fell
deep, drowning,
in the dark
sea of insanity.

he wasn't mine
he wasn't even his own

he
belonged
to
a
sea
of
creatures
who
controlled
him

on the days where he
remembered me,
my skin tingled as
if ants crawled all
over my body.

beauty of our minds
and the things
that are not seen

fascinated by the
thoughts of us
and all the love
we once shared

but there was
a whirlwind
of our destruction

and although i
felt incapable
of moving on

i did

my tears created an ocean
and one day i swam
through that ocean
and made it to shore

- on my own without you

a light bulb
had turned on
a g a i n

he was no longer
a need but a want.

- society standards subconsciously working my brain

my mother always
taught me to be
independent and
not count on a man
for anything.

"en caso de"
"just in case"

she would say to me,

teaching me that
i can still be a
Puerto Rican Woman
without the needs
of a man because
i would never
be an other.

i refused to be othered
by his past.
we needed to be one
and the same.
and if we could not be
the same, then it'd
be best i walk away.

mujer latina
mujer virtuosa

- gracias mami

we were in the middle of
a carnival surrounded by
so many people and children,
i felt anxiety on my fingertips
with so many beings around.

suddenly, he turned around,
looked at me, centimeters away
from my face. he breathed me
in and i thought we were
infinite in those seconds.

life has a way of fucking
with you because the ferris wheel
was like our life.

looking
from
high up
above
everything
looks
perfect

till you hit rock bottom and get off the ride.

love does not equal hurt.
love is an amazing thing
to feel, to hold, to cherish;
it's usually the who and what
behind the love that cause
the
pain.

don't blame love;
blame the who or the what
for lying to you
for making you believe
that love is ~~pain~~
love ~~hurts~~

- you should experience love with the right person,
  not the wrong one

i'm sorry that no one
taught you how to
appreciate someone.
i'm sorry that the females
before me tainted you.
i'm sorry that i had to
pay for their actions.

- the never ending cycle of abuse

although he wasn't dead,
i still grieved him.
the love of my life
was no longer a part
of my life.

- sorrow

i woke up
in the morning
mourning you

- welcome to the new year

it sucks when
they want to
make it work,
and it's too late
and your mind
has been tattered,
and your heart's
already broken.

the ones who break your heart,
can't repair it either.

- a permanent fixture

there were days
that he made
me feel like
a worthless
piece of shit.

was i a last
minute
decision
in order not
to make me
feel bad?

i couldn't place my
time and energy
on that relationship.

he created violence
deep in the wells
of my stomach
where cancer
once existed

i revolted
the notion
of having
poison
inside
my body

oh sense of smell how i
cannot stand you sometimes.
you bring the best and worst
memories to life.

walking through the streets
a stranger with his cologne
a laundry mat with his detergent

memories of laughter
memories of reckless abandon
memories of us withering away

- nostalgia has a way of creeping up
  on you when you least expect it

sometimes guilt circled
me like a dark cloud
for leaving him.

the dark clouds are
the demons that loved
confinement of the
emotional abuse.

everything was in slow
motion one day and for
a moment i swore my
soul looked at my body
and i wondered looking
at myself, how did i lose
myself all for a man who
doesn't know how to love me?

- i was unrecognizable

the ghost of
my past self
haunted me.

she had done
so much better,
reminding me

"you can get through anything"

i unlearned
the suffering
and untangled
myself from the
vines of my heart

the rage fired up inside
me like a forest creating
more fire of
everything i once knew
that was me and him

and the ashes were filled
of bitterness and hate and
upset and irritation and anger

because i wasted so much
time on a person that never
deserved one second of me

and in that moment i decided
to save myself from the torment
that lived within me

i took the ashes from the
forest and threw them in
the ocean

i went back to the forest
and planted sunflowers
of love and happiness
and joy and forgiveness and
peace of mind and me

the remedy of healing
was in the fire he
made out of me.

the remedy was not
in the wine i tried
diving myself into
every night.

i never wanted to
settle with pain

deep down inside me
a passionate woman existed

i owed it to myself
to bring the best
out of me

i have a mason jar
full of small little
love notes he gifted
me one day

on the days i
questioned his love
for me, i would
look through those
small little love notes

i
found
nothing

but an array of illusion

have you ever felt
like someone is
literally squeezing
your heart?

"it hurts"
"it hurts"
"it hurts"

crying it out in the shower
screaming it to my pillow
writing it out on paper

and on the days
that i long him,

my nights remind me
of why i don't want him.

the haunting truth
of reality
is a nightmare that
visits me frequently.

he was only two inches
away from me when i
woke up having a
nightmare about him.
i looked at him
while he slept.

i wondered
how
he
could
sleep
so
soundly
with a tornado
laying beside him.

i wondered
if in his
sleep he
felt the chaos
burning within me.

there was a war
going on within my
   body
        soul
mind
     and
          heart

composing
myself like
music, i
synchronized
my body
my soul
my mind
and my heart
to one tune

making a melody
out of all the parts
i let him take out
of sequence

i
can
do
so
much
better
than
this

these words were
the calcium my
bones needed

lovesick:

i
was
sick
of
being
so
in
love
with
him

i have been
irrevocably
changed
by this man

and i am
grateful
for all the
insight he
gave me
of myself

i would wish
him the best
goodbyes with
someone else

but i couldn't
stand the thought
of him being with
someone else

- hope in him

i forgive you for
hurting me when
you didn't even know it.
for nesting in me
feelings of despair.

- growing hope within myself instead

i started thinking
about my life
without him and
making plans for
myself that didn't
include him in it.

i started feeling
optimistic
for me and this
life of mine.

- to all the 11:11's we stopped wishing on

i learned to
stop waiting
for him.

my goals were
on the other
side waiting to
be reached.

with
or
without
him

all the love
i had inside
me, i gave it
to him.

and when we
were over,
i learned to
give others
that love.

the love inside
me would've
driven me to
the brink.

because
i
was
born
out
of
love

the most dangerous
humans are the
women who realize
they don't need
anyone after facing
the hurricane alone

to him, i was
his muse.

but i really
think he was
my muse.

he created
p o e t r y
out of me.

i learned that life lets you
meet people in order to
find yourself

and sometimes you just
come out stronger than
before because that's
what life wanted out
of you.

a
better
person

don't ever wait on
someone to reach
your full potential.
you go.
make your moves.
be your own team.
be your own queen.
live in a castle and
still build an empire.
and keep it moving
with your head up high.

you
got
this

love will make you
do crazy things.
it's true.
love will make you
see connections
that don't even exist.

you're trying to
convince yourself
of something
that isn't real.

do not turn bitter
oh beautiful goddess

write, cry, sing,
paint, draw, feel
with all your pain.
make it into beautiful art.

but oh you beautiful
creature, i beg of you
to not turn your heart
into stone.

asking "what do you want from me?"
is handing control over to someone,
when you have control over your
own life.

what
is it
that
you
want?

yank that control back like
the queen you are and make
sure they see that crown
while you take back what's yours,

your life
your body
your soul

become
a
warrior
again

you were born one anyway.

how long will you wade
for the lover who doesn't swim
through storms for you?

it's okay to miss
that person.

it's okay to cry
in the most random times.

it's okay to still love
even after all the madness.

you
have
every
right
to
feel.

fuck anyone who tells you otherwise.

while you read your books,
characters will remind you of them.
quotes will speak life upon that
once relationship. and in that
moment take a deep breath,
notice your worth,
and release that breath of stardust.

you come first.

every
single
time

there will be times
when you look at
other couples
holding hands
kissing
loving one another
and you will feel loss.

it's
all
part
of
the
process

reminder:
it is worthwhile
to be single,
rather than to be
with someone who
continuously takes
you for granted.

don't waste time
regretting the
time you wasted

you
can
never
take
back
time

make time for
yourself now

rub self care on like oil

some
answers
to your
questions
will
never
be
answered.

there are things
in that very
moment of space
and time,
you aren't supposed
to understand.

accept time
like a friend,
and everything
else will fall through.

put
distance
between
you
and
them

stop answering their every text
unfollow them on all sites

you
need
to
heal

- healing is better when they are a planet away

stop trying to change
someone that doesn't
want to change.

you can't do everything
for someone. if that person
cannot find themselves,
then let go.

because without you
even knowing it,
you're letting go of yourself.

you're so beautiful
and i hope you
know that.

you hid all your
insecurities behind
the person who complimented
you every single day.

and now that this person
is gone, you ask yourself
if you're still beautiful.
if the sun shines.
if someone else will
notice the scars and beauty marks
this person once counted.

a
kindly
reminder:
you're magical

stop romanticizing
this dark crazy love
with someone while
they trigger your mental illness.

there's
nothing
romantic
about
someone
fucking
you
mentally

sometimes people come
into your life for a moment
to rekindle a flame that
was once put out.
and once that burning
fire returns, they leave.

- they already did their part in your life.

you will find passions
that will grow fruits
of amazingness

your belly will grow
with babies of
stability
confidence
and kindness

nurture these things

you
will
glow

when he sees this

do
not
let
him
back
in

tell him with your silence that he can go fuck himself

one day you
will look back
and be so
happy that your
heart break is over
the suffering is over
the wait is over

and those days
will come and go

you are made of
power and strength

do you paint the sky
familiar with what
you know?

or do you color
something that has
not been born yet?

imagination has
a way of telling you
how you really feel.

nourish
what
hasn't
been
born
yet

you were made out of
stardust
and that's why lovers
don't understand you,
because you have galaxies
of life, love, and wildness
living inside you.

they weren't ready
to see that shooting
star spread like wildfire
throughout the sky

do not look for me
in other people.

i
do
not
exist
elsewhere

and when you meet another,
do not mention my name nor
keep me in your memory.

for surely you will try to find me
in her but you will not be satisfied.
forget me.
and make sure she doesn't read this book.

i found myself
in an island
of thoughts
surrounded by
waves of
positivity.

this time
the moon
shined bright
on my skin
and i
finally
danced.

- alone in the sand of self acceptance

there were two
roads that led
me to different
destinies.

the road of self destruction.
the road of self love.

i packed my bags
and took the
self love route.

i told my ghost to
meet me at the castle,
we were going
to have a chat.

sometimes you need
to talk to yourself
and make decisions
without counting
on anyone if it's
right or wrong.

parts of a memoir that he wrote for me:

"her smile is the first thing i think of when i wake up in the mornings. i hear her laughs throughout my day, phantom laughs, laughs i may never hear again, eyes i may never gaze into, lips i may never kiss, and hands i may never hold. she taught me so much in the time we've been together. act on something instead of just speaking about it is probably one of the biggest lessons. i wonder if she learned anything positive from me but i know i caused her so much pain, i don't think she could've walked away with much positive."

i
turned
all
your
negatives
into
positives

i found
beauty
in my
brokenness

i found
self love
in my
darkness

although he created poetry
out of me, it also broke us.

- like this next poem

dear pretty little thing,

stop crying for the boy
who couldn't love you
the way you deserve
to be loved.

like the delicate flower you are.
like the storm you are.
like the everything you are.

you
are
the
universe
pretty little thing.

and he can't love you enough
because he doesn't know
what to do with the universe
he's holding in his hands.

sometimes you can't teach
someone how to love.
you are not his mother,
pretty little thing.
you were once his lover.

you were meant to be loved by a lover.
not a son in search of his mother.

and if there is
one thing i learned
in all of this is that
there will always be
love, and you
will always be
the one i'm
thankful for,
because you
handed me the stars
without knowing it.
and you handed
me an anchor to
keep myself at bay.

- the end

thank you to the humans
who knew about this book
and never asked me why.
why i wrote about our story
instead of the other stories.

thank you to the book
community for supporting
my poetry since the beginning
of my blog. i found sisters
and brothers in you.

thank you to the humans
who love and love and love.

you know who you are.

- acknowledgements

you can find me here:
blog: chicnerdreads.wordpress.com
twitter: chicnerdreads
instagram: chicnerdreads
tumblr: chicnerdreads.tumblr.com

Made in the USA
San Bernardino, CA
26 December 2017